S0-BAP-489

SOJOURNER TRUTH

and the Voice of Freedom

by Jane Shumate

SOUTH HUNTINGTON
PUBLIC LIBRARY
2 MELVILLE ROAD
HUNTINGTON STATION, N.Y. 11746

Gateway Civil Rights
The Millbrook Press
Brookfield, Connecticut

Interior Design: Tilman Reitzle

Photographs courtesy of: Warner Collection, Gulf States
Paper Corporation: cover; Steele Collection: cover inset, 2-3, 10,
16, 17, 24; Schomburg Center for Research in Black Culture: 1, 8,
11, 15, 29; Detroit Historical Museum: 4; Chicago Historical
Society: 7; New-York Historical Society: 12, 22; Library of
Congress: 18-19, 27; Sophia Smith Collection: 21; Neil Drake: 28;
Sojourner Truth Library, New Paltz, New York: 30.

Cataloging-in-Publication Data

Shumate, Jane
Sojourner Truth and the voice of freedom.

32 pp.; ill.: (Gateway Civil Rights)
Bibliography: p.
Includes index.

Summary: Sojourner Truth dedicated her life to achieving
equal rights for blacks and women. Her courage, drive, and
speaking talent inspired many people. This tall, deep-voiced
former slave helped plant the seeds of equal rights for all.

1. Truth, Sojourner, 1797-1883. 2. Afro-Americans–Biography.
3. Abolitionists. 4. Reformers.
1991 B (92) Truth
ISBN 1-56294-041-4

Copyright © 1991 by Jane Shumate
All rights reserved
Printed in the United States of America
6 5 4 3 2 1

444426   B-4687

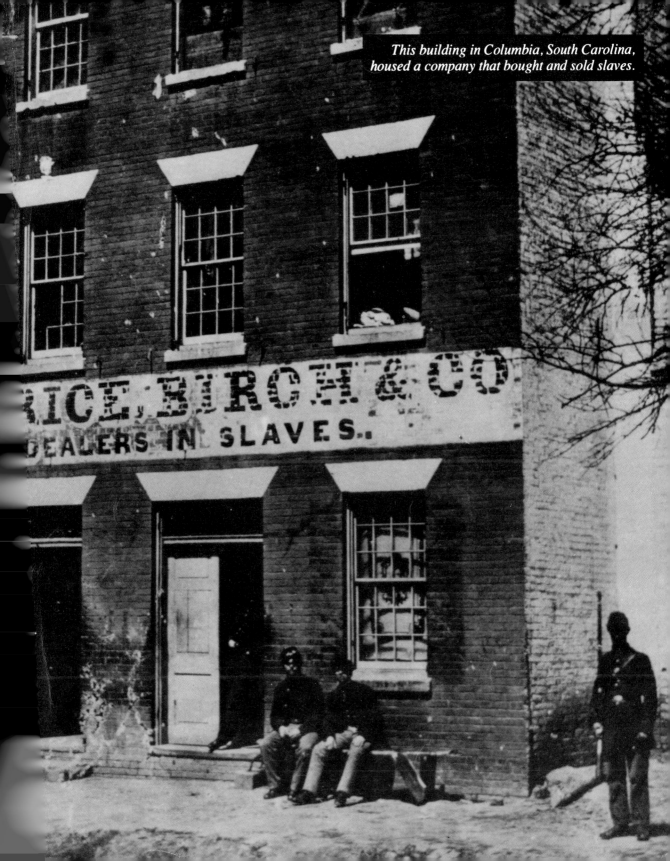

This building in Columbia, South Carolina, housed a company that bought and sold slaves.

One day in 1852, a noisy group of people gathered in a lecture hall in Akron, Ohio. They had come to hear speeches about human rights. When a tall figure appeared on the stage, a stunned silence fell over the audience. In the next instant, the crowd exploded, shouting twice as loudly as before.

The people were shocked because the figure on stage was a black woman. Women almost never spoke in public. And for a black woman to address an audience—why, it was incredible!

But this woman soon had the whole crowd listening to her deep, powerful voice. She talked about civil rights. Many people were concerned about the rights of blacks, especially the black slaves in the South. But this woman spoke about the rights of all people—black and white, men and women.

"Well, children," she said, "where there is so much racket, there must be something out of kilter. I think that between the Negroes of the South, and the women of the North, all talking about rights, the white men will be in a fix pretty soon!"

When the black woman finished speaking, the audience roared its approval. She spoke what many people felt in their hearts.

This woman, whose name was Sojourner Truth, knew what it was like to live without basic human rights. She was born a slave and had

Sojourner Truth met President Abraham Lincoln, who called her Aunty Sojourner.

been bought, sold, and beaten many times in her life. She could not read or write. Yet she became one of the most famous black women of her time, known throughout the country as a powerful activist for equal rights. She was so famous that she knew President Abraham Lincoln, who called her Aunty Sojourner. Her story is one of the most courageous in the history of civil rights.

Isabella

Sojourner Truth was born in New York State, in about 1797, as a slave for a Dutch family called the Hardenberghs. Her name then was Isabella, for she didn't change it until she was much older. Her parents were named Mau-Mau Bett and Baumfree. Like the Hardenberghs, Isabella and her parents did not speak English. They spoke a language called Low Dutch.

Slavery was legal all over America at that time, and slaves were still being brought from Africa and the West Indies. Isabella and her family lived as many slaves did in those days. They worked hard from morning until night. Then they slept with nine other people in one room, on straw on the floor. This room was dark, damp, and smelly. When it rained, the floor turned into mud.

Isabella's parents had many other children, but all except Isabella and her little brother had been sold to new owners. Isabella often found her mother in tears, thinking of her children and remembering how they had cried when they were taken away. Mau-Mau Bett taught Isabella to obey her master and work hard, so she wouldn't be beaten. She also taught her to have hope, to be honest, and to pray to God. Mau-Mau Bett said that God would help her if she told him her troubles. Isabella always remembered this, and she often had long "talks" with God.

When Isabella was 9, her master died. His heirs sold much of his property, including his slaves, for the slaves were treated the same as cows and sheep. Slave buyers did not care about keeping slave families together. Isabella was sold to one family called the Nealys, and her

Isabella's family was sold at an auction like this one.

brother was sold to another. Baumfree was too old and sick to work anymore, so he was set free. Mau-Mau Bett was set free to take care of him.

When Isabella was led away by her new masters she was scared and lonely. She had never been apart from her family. Besides, the Nealys spoke English, while Isabella spoke Low Dutch. She tried to learn English, but nobody helped her. The Nealys did not understand Isabella's confusion, and they whipped her when she made mistakes. Isabella often had talks with God about this and asked him for a new master.

While Isabella was living with the Nealys, her mother fell ill and died. Isabella's father needed to be cared for. The Nealys wouldn't let Isabella leave to nurse her father. He had nothing to eat and no way to keep warm, so he soon died, too.

In 1808, the slave trade was outlawed in the United States. It was no longer legal to buy slaves from other countries, but people still bought and sold slaves within the United States. In 1809, Isabella was sold to a man named Dumont. She was 12 years old. By then she was strong and tall, and she worked very hard. Dumont said that she was worth more than a man because she did a man's work in the day and a woman's work at night.

Isabella thought that slavery was honorable. She liked to please her

NEGROES FOR SALE.

☞ Will be sold at public auction, at Spring Hill, in the County of Hempstead, on a credit of twelve months, on Friday the 28th day of this present month, 15 young and valuable Slaves, consisting of 9 superior Men & Boys, between 12 and 27 years of age, one woman about 43 years who is a good washer and cook, one woman about twenty-seven, and one very likely young woman with three children.

Also at the same time, and on the same terms, three Mules, about forty head of Cattle, plantation tools, one waggon, and a first rate Gin stand, manufactured by Pratt &Co.

Bond with two or more approved securities will be required. Sale to commence at 10 o'clock.

E. E. Hundley,
W. Robinson,
H. M. Robinson.

Posters advertised auctions at which human beings were sold.

master. She imagined that he was a god and was always watching her. But most of all Isabella thought that if she worked hard she would earn her freedom.

When Isabella was about 17, her master married her to a slave named Thomas, who was also owned by the Dumonts. They were not legally married, though, because slaves did not have that right. They were just allowed to live together as husband and wife. Masters liked their slaves to "marry" and have children because then they would own more slaves. Isabella and Thomas had five children altogether: Diana, Elizabeth, Hannah, Peter, and Sophie. Isabella was proud to give her master so many children.

Emancipation!

In 1824, Isabella heard some wondrous news. New York State had passed an emancipation, or freedom, law. One by one, northern states were making slavery illegal. The new law meant that Isabella would be freed on July 4, 1827. Her prayers had been answered! Later, Dumont told her that if she worked especially hard he would free her one year earlier. It seemed that her hard work *would* pay off! Isabella was overjoyed.

She worked days and nights, chopping wood and hauling water and harvesting corn and spinning wool, even though she had her own children to tend to as well. She worked so hard that she hurt her hand badly. That didn't stop her. But when the time came in 1826, Dumont

Slaves were forced to work long days in the fields.

refused to free her. He said that her injury had stopped her from keeping her part of the bargain.

That day was a turning point for Isabella. She had never lied, or stolen, or disobeyed her master. But he had broken his word to her. What he did was not just. Isabella suddenly saw how wrong slavery was. She decided that since she was not given her freedom, she would take it herself. She bundled together some food and clothes, picked up her baby, Sophie, kissed the older children good-bye while they slept, and tiptoed away before dawn.

But where would she go? She had not thought about what she would do once she was free. A friend told her to go to the house of a couple named the Van Wageners. They were Quakers, people whose religion taught them that slavery was wrong. They were happy to take in Isabella and her baby.

"I Will Have My Child Again!"

Isabella was content living with the Van Wageners, and she worked hard to repay their kindness. But she missed her other children. According to the emancipation law, they would be Dumont's slaves until they were adults. Then she heard some terrible news: Her son, Peter, had been sold to a planter in Alabama. This meant that he would never be free, for in the South there was no emancipation law.

Isabella was stunned, but she soon decided to act. She would try to get her son back. She declared, "I will have my child again!"

Isabella's Quaker friends told her that she had the right to file a lawsuit demanding that Peter be returned to her. It could be very difficult for Isabella to do this. Most people did not believe that a black woman would try to sue a white man. But her friends gave her money and sent her to a good lawyer. She worked hard for

Isabella was a determined woman.

New York City in the early 1800s.

months. Finally, she won back her boy and rescued him from slavery. Isabella was the first black in New York, and one of the first black women in the country, to win a suit against a white man.

At about this time, Isabella began to go to the Methodist Church. The people at church were very impressed by her. She was strong and determined—and six feet tall! And she had a powerful voice. When she sang or spoke, they all listened. One woman, Miss Gear, encouraged her to move with Peter to New York City, where many freed slaves were finding opportunities. So, in 1829, Isabella took Sophie back to Dumont's estate to leave her in the care of her other children. Then she and Peter moved to New York.

"The Kingdom"

Isabella and Peter were thrilled when they reached New York. It was the first big, bustling city they had ever seen, and they were amazed by the crowds and the speeding carriages and all the noise. There, Miss

Gear put Peter in a navigation school, where he would learn to become a sailor, and she found Isabella a job working for a family. Isabella joined the Zion African Church, where she soon became known for her beautiful songs and prayers.

Isabella also worked at a place called the Magdalene Asylum, which took care of homeless women. The asylum was directed by a man named Elijah Pierson. He was a kind man, but he had strange religious beliefs. He became involved with another man who had even stranger beliefs. The two declared that they were God and God's prophet. They asked people to believe in them, give them money, and work on their farm, which they called The Kingdom.

Isabella liked Mr. Pierson and his friend, and she believed them. In about 1832, she became one of the men's followers. She gave them all her money and worked for nothing. But soon she saw that they were tricking her. She left "The Kingdom" and returned to the city. But then a terrible thing happened. Mr. Pierson died mysteriously, and some people accused Isabella of poisoning him. Isabella was innocent. She remembered that she had rights. She sued the people who accused her, and she won.

"The Rich Rob the Poor, and the Poor Rob One Another"

For a while, Isabella worked quietly for a family in New York. During this time, Peter got into trouble. He was running with a bad crowd, and he lied and stole. He even went to jail. In 1839, Peter decided to leave New York. A friend helped him get a job on a whaling ship. Isabella was sad to see her son go, but she decided it was for the best. Although Peter wrote to his mother occasionally, Isabella never saw him again.

Isabella's son was gone now, and she had had some bad experiences in New York. She began to feel that the city was full of evil. People were selfish and got each other into trouble. "The rich rob the poor," she said, "and the poor rob one another." But Isabella had also learned that she had a talent: People listened when she spoke to them in her deep and powerful voice. It seemed to her that God wanted her to go out and speak to people and tell them to be just and have hope. So in 1843 Isabella left New York City to become a traveling preacher. She was going to spread the word of God.

Sojourner Truth

Before setting out, Isabella changed her name. She decided that it was not right for a preacher to have the name of a slave. "When I left the house of bondage," she said, "I left everything behind." She decided to call herself "Sojourner," which means traveler, and "Truth," because she was going to preach the Gospel.

Wherever Sojourner Truth went, she talked to people. She talked about God and religion and how people should treat each other well. She had clever ways of saying things. People were impressed by this witty, rich-voiced black woman. News of her spread, and people would

This poster advertises one of Sojourner Truth's talks about human rights.

I Sell the Shadow to Support the Substance.
SOJOURNER TRUTH.

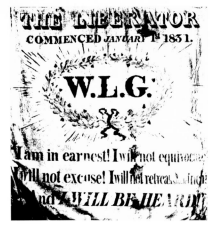

The title page of The Liberator.

come a long way to hear her powerful speeches.

In her travels, Sojourner met a group of people in Massachusetts who lived together in a community called the Northampton Association of Education and Industry. These people believed in equal rights. They respected each other's opinions, even if they disagreed.

Sojourner stayed with them until 1846. There she met many interesting people, including the abolitionists Frederick Douglass and William Lloyd Garrison, editor of the abolitionist newspaper *The Liberator*. The abolitionists believed that slavery was wrong. Douglass and Garrison encouraged Sojourner to speak about slavery on her speaking tours.

Over the next few years Sojourner traveled and spoke often against slavery. Many Northerners tried to ignore slavery. They said that it was a Southern problem, now that most slaves in the North were free. But Sojourner couldn't forget all those black people who were still being whipped or taken away from their families.

She decided to publish a book describing her life as a slave, to make people understand how terrible slavery was. But she could not write or read, so a friend wrote the story for her. In 1850, *The Narrative of Sojourner Truth* was published. People read about how little Isabella's family was split up and how her parents died. They became more convinced that slavery in the South would have to end.

Frederick Douglass

Frederick Douglass was born a slave on a Maryland plantation in about 1818. When he was 7 years old, he was given an unusual opportunity: He was taught to read and write. His master was angry when he found out, so Douglass realized how powerful education must be. When he was 20, he escaped to Massachusetts.

There, he began to attend antislavery meetings. Soon he was speaking out against slavery himself. He talked about politics and expressed himself in complex ideas. White people had never seen a black man like him. Soon he caught the attention of abolitionists such as William Lloyd Garrison, and in 1841 he joined the Massachusetts Antislavery Society.

In 1845, he wrote *The Narrative and Life of Frederick Douglass*. It was read by thousands of people. He also published newspapers about equal rights for blacks and women. He urged blacks to get an education and vote. He also helped about 400 Southern slaves escape slavery.

When the Civil War broke out, Douglass encouraged freed blacks to fight for the North and help win freedom for all. Douglass's two sons fought in an all-black Massachusetts regiment.

Even after the war was over and slavery was abolished, Douglass kept working. He fought discrimination until he died, in 1895.

Poverty and suffering are etched into the faces of this slave family.

Sojourner took copies of her book with her wherever she went and sold them to her audiences. Now she had another way to spread the truth. She also had a way to make some money. She hoped one day to buy a home of her own where she could bring her children to live with her.

In the early 1850s, Sojourner began to talk about women's rights, too. At that time, women in the United States could not vote or hold elective office. Sojourner believed that all people—black and white, men and women—had been created equal and should have the same rights and receive the same treatment. She couldn't see why anyone should have more rights than she did.

Sojourner told people exactly how she felt. At the National Women's Rights Convention in 1850, she said, "If women want any rights more than they's got, why don't they just take them, and not be talking about it?" That was what *she* had always done!

"Sojourner, Free Speech, and the Union!"

But it was not so easy. Many people didn't want women to have equal rights or slaves to be free. They thought that white men were the natural leaders of society, and that blacks and women should not expect equal status.

In the 1850s, people's opinions about equal rights grew stronger. In the South, where there were many large plantations, white people relied on slaves. The slaves worked on the plantations, and whites said they

The Early
Women's Movement

Elizabeth Cady Stanton

In the 1830s, many northern women were abolitionists. They helped slaves to escape, and they organized antislavery meetings and printed antislavery pamphlets. Their goals were to end slavery and to help blacks get equal rights.

While helping blacks, these women began to think about themselves. They weren't full citizens either. They couldn't vote. When they got married, their property became their husbands'. If they had jobs, they weren't paid the same as men.

In 1848, two women abolitionists, Elizabeth Cady Stanton and Lucretia Mott, organized the first convention for women's rights at Seneca Falls, New York. Hundreds of women—and men—came. The Seneca Falls Declaration of Rights and Sentiments demanded that women be given full citizenship and the right to vote.

Many more conventions followed, including the ones at which Sojourner Truth spoke. Women printed pamphlets and had people sign petitions, which they took to state governments. They convinced some states to grant women individual rights and to allow them to have better jobs.

Women finally won the right to vote—but not until 1920.

The Civil War brought four years of bloody battles.

could not get the crops harvested without them. In the North, farms were smaller, so people there didn't rely as much on slaves. Many Northerners wanted slavery outlawed everywhere. Southerners wanted the right to make their own laws. The disagreement grew stronger year by year. It seemed that the Union might split in two.

In 1857, Sojourner Truth moved to a town near Battle Creek, Michigan. She had saved enough money to buy a little house. Her daughters were free women now, and soon they moved there too. Sojourner felt that she had a real home at last.

Soon afterwards, Sojourner set out on a speaking tour to try to convince people that the slavery issue could be ended peacefully. Many people became angry with her and tried to stop her. She was even arrested when she went to speak in Indiana, a state that free blacks were forbidden to enter. But she had many supporters there who cheered, "Sojourner, Free Speech, and the Union!"

War, however, could not be stopped. It broke out on April 12, 1861, when Southern troops fired on Fort Sumter in South Carolina.

Aunty Sojourner Truth

The Civil War, between the Confederate army of the South and the Union army of the North, lasted four years. Battles raged all over the country and took heavy tolls. In 1863, one of the war's most terrible battles was fought. In the battle of Gettysburg, 45,000 men died in just three days of fighting. Both sides suffered terrible losses, and even those who weren't fighting in the war felt the pain of losing their sons, husbands, or fathers.

The Civil War raged for so long that many began to fear it would never end. Sojourner told her listeners to be patient. She said, "It takes a great while to turn about this great ship of state."

Changes were made bit by bit. In 1862, President Lincoln announced the Emancipation Proclamation, which freed slaves in the South. Many of these slaves joined the Northern army to help finish the war. One black man who joined the army was Sojourner's grandson. Sojourner visited the black troops to cheer them on.

In 1864, Sojourner Truth traveled to Washington. She was very well known by then, and she was able to get into the White House to see President Lincoln. She told him that he was the best president the country had ever had—but she also admitted that she hadn't heard of him before he ran for president. Lincoln smiled and replied, "I had heard of you many times before that." He signed a book she carried with her, "For Aunty Sojourner Truth, A. Lincoln, Oct. 29, 1864." This was Sojourner Truth's proudest moment.

Thousands of former slaves traveled northward after the Civil War.

In early 1865, after 600,000 people had been killed in the fighting, the Northern troops were finally victorious and the Civil War ended. The Thirteenth Amendment was passed, banning slavery forever.

There was still work to do, though, to rebuild the Union. Now that blacks were free, they needed help finding jobs, building homes, and starting new lives. But before President Lincoln could lay plans to help the freed blacks, he was assassinated. His death shocked the country. Black people grieved especially, for Abraham Lincoln had been the most important person in helping them gain their freedom. They were counting on him to help them build new lives, and they wondered what would happen now that he was gone.

"I WANT TO RIDE!"

Sojourner Truth knew that many blacks would need help in their new lives, for she remembered how lost and confused she had felt when she first escaped from slavery. She began to work in Washington for the National Freedmen's Relief Association. She taught freed slaves how to take care of themselves, how to find jobs, and how to demand their rights.

Her next job was with the Freedmen's Hospital, where she made sure that blacks were given proper health care. She often had to travel across the city with heavy bundles of supplies. By this time, Sojourner was nearly 70, and it was hard for her to walk far. Black people were allowed to ride the streetcar, but only in special sections. This made Sojourner angry, and she complained to the president of the streetcar company. As a result, a new law was passed permitting blacks to ride wherever they wanted.

But many streetcar conductors did not obey the new law. They didn't want to give rides to black people at all. One day, a conductor wouldn't stop to pick up Sojourner. She ran after him and shouted, "I WANT TO RIDE!" She was an old woman, but she had such a strong voice that people stopped in the middle of the road and blocked the streetcar so she could get on.

Another time, a conductor tried to shove her off the train, and he hurt her shoulder badly. Sojourner sued him and had him fired from his job. Soon blacks were riding the streetcar as freely as whites.

Sojourner ended the segregation of streetcars in Washington and made a difference in the lives of many blacks. She was pleased with this victory, but she also saw that much work needed to be done before blacks would be treated as full citizens.

The Last Crusade

Sojourner had an idea. Why not give blacks some land in the West, so they could set up communities and learn to be farmers? This seemed fair. After all, for many years black people had worked for nothing, and they had even helped win the war.

With help, Sojourner drew up a petition asking Congress to grant portions of western land to blacks. In 1870, she set out on a tour to convince people to sign her petition.

Before beginning her tour, Sojourner made an important visit in Washington. This time she met President Ulysses S. Grant and went to the United States Senate. The same woman who had once been beaten by slave owners was now cheered by a hall full of senators!

Sojourner traveled throughout the country, from Massachusetts to Michigan to Kansas, lecturing to people and convincing them to sign her petition. Thousands agreed with her that blacks should be given land in the West, and they signed their names.

After several years of touring and gathering names, Sojourner returned with her petition to Washington, and she presented it to Congress. But the Congressmen did not vote in favor of the petition to give blacks land in the West. They seemed to think that if blacks were no longer enslaved, that was enough. They refused to go so far as to offer blacks land to start new lives.

Sojourner could see that the equal rights movement was just beginning. It would take more than a proclamation or an amendment for black people to be truly free. Many white people would have to change their racist attitudes. Many black people would have to be taught what to do with their freedom. And there was much work to do in the fight for women's rights.

Sojourner devoted the last part of her life to women's rights. Now that black men could vote, she wanted to help women win the right to vote, too. She said, "If colored men get their rights, and not colored women theirs, you see the colored men will be masters over the women, and it will be just as bad as it was before."

By this time, Sojourner's sight and hearing had grown weak, and she needed a cane to walk. She still believed strongly in women's rights, but she was los-

Black men won the right to vote in 1870.

ing the physical strength to carry on the struggle. Nevertheless, she still had the spirit. "I am about 80 years old," she said. "I have been 40 years a slave and 40 years free, and would be here 40 years more to have equal rights for all."

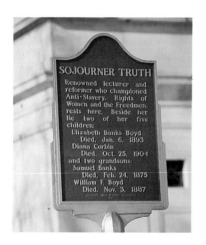

This plaque marks Sojourner Truth's grave in Battle Creek, Michigan.

Sojourner stopped traveling outside of her home state of Michigan. She still lectured in Michigan, though. In 1878, she visited and spoke in almost 40 towns.

Sojourner spent her last years quietly with her family at her home near Battle Creek. In 1883, after a long illness, she died. More than a thousand people, including many of the famous abolitionists and women's rights activists of her day, came to her funeral to pay their respects.

Sojourner Truth dedicated her life to achieving equal rights. Her courage, drive, and speaking talent inspired many people. This tall, deep-voiced former slave helped plant the seeds of equal rights for all.

Important Dates in the Life of Sojourner Truth

1797?	Isabella Hardenbergh is born in Ulster County, New York.
1827	Isabella is legally freed by New York's emancipation law.
1829	Isabella and her son Peter move to New York City.
1843	Isabella changes her name to Sojourner Truth and begins preaching.
1850	*The Narrative of Sojourner Truth* is published.
1857	Sojourner moves to a house near Battle Creek, Michigan.
1864	Sojourner meets President Abraham Lincoln. She begins to work in Washington, D.C.
1865	The Thirteenth Amendment is passed, abolishing slavery.
1870	Sojourner meets President Ulysses S. Grant and visits the U.S. Senate.
1883	Sojourner Truth dies in Michigan on November 26.

FIRST DAY OF ISSU

Find Out More About Sojourner Truth

Books: *Frederick Douglass: Freedom Fighter* by Lillie
Patterson (Champaign, Ill.: Garrard, 1965).

Her Name Was Sojourner Truth by Hertha Pauli (New
York: Appleton-Century Crofts, 1962).

Sojourner Truth and the Struggle for Freedom by
Edward Beecher Claflin (New York: Barrons, 1987).

Women of America: Susan B. Anthony by Cindy Klingel
(Mankato, Minn.: Creative Education, 1987).

Places: In the Detroit Historical Museum there is a painting of
Sojourner Truth with President Abraham Lincoln.

Sojourner Truth's grave is in Oakhill Cemetery, Battle
Creek, Michigan. It is marked by a granite tombstone
and a historical sign.

The Sojourner Truth commemorative stamp was issued in 1986.

Index

SOUTH HUNTINGTON PL

0652 9100 013 502 3

DISCARDED

jB
TRUTH

Shumate, Jane

Sojourner Truth and
the voice of
freedom

$11.90   444426

DATE			

FEB 1 1 1992

SOUTH HUNTINGTON
PUBLIC LIBRARY
2 MELVILLE ROAD
HUNTINGTON STATION, N.Y. 11746

BAKER & TAYLOR BOOKS